Look for the Rainbow

LOOK
FOR THE
RAINBOW

Words of

Sympathy and Faith

Selected by

Lois Daniel

Illustrated With

Beautiful

Color Photographs

HALLMARK EDITIONS

"Mary Is a Net Gain" by William Allen White. Reprinted by permission of W. L. White. "A New Horizon" by Billy Graham from *Reader's Digest* (April 1971). Reprinted by permission of Fred Dienert. "Faith" from *Shadowed Valley*, by Hyman Judah Schachtel. Copyright © 1962 by Hyman Judah Schachtel. Reprinted by permission of Alfred A. Knopf, Inc. "The Larger Truth" from *On Reflection* by Helen Hayes. Copyright © 1968 by Helen Hayes and Sandford Dody. Published by M. Evans and Company, Inc., 216 East 49 Street, New York. "Of Joy and Sorrow" from *The Prophet*, by Kahlil Gibran. Copyright 1923 by Kahlil Gibran; renewal copyright 1951 by Administrators C. T. A. of Kahlil Gibran Estate and Mary G. Gibran. Reprinted by permission of Alfred A. Knopf, Inc. "Prayer" from *The Heart of Peter Marshall's Faith* compiled by Catherine Marshall. Copyright 1949, 1950, 1956 by Fleming H. Revell Company. Used by permission. "The Night Is Not Dark" from the High Holy Day Message of The Jewish Theological Seminary of America. Used by permission. Excerpt from "It Helps If I'm Cheerful," by Rose Kennedy, *Life* Magazine, July 17, 1970, © 1970 Time Inc. "An Open Letter" from the book *Up The Golden Stair* by Elizabeth Yates. Copyright © 1966 by Elizabeth Yates McGreal. Published by E.P. Dutton & Co., Inc., and used with their permission. "The Good Fridays of Life" from *My Life With Martin Luther King, Jr.*, by Coretta Scott King. Copyright © 1969. Holt, Rinehart and Winston, Inc., publishers. "Invitation" from *The Healing of Sorrow* by Norman Vincent Peale. Copyright 1966, Inspirational Book Service, Pawling, N.Y. "Mourning" reprinted with permission. From *A Grief Observed* by C.S. Lewis. Copyright 1961 by N.W. Clerk. Published in the United States of America by The Seabury Press, Inc., New York. "A New Perspective" from *On Eternity* by George and Helen Papashvily in *Words To Live By.* Copyright 1945, 1946, 1947, 1948 by William J. Nichols. Reprinted by permission of Simon and Schuster, Inc. "No Other Way" from *Half Way Up The Mountain* by Martha Smock. Copyright 1971 Unity School of Christianity, Unity Village, Mo. "Winter Heart" by Mildred Meeker from *A Treasury of Unity Poems.* Copyright 1964 Unity School of Christianity, Unity Village, Mo. "Wings" by Rowena Cheney from *Ibid.* "Life Is Good" by Eleanor Halbrook Zimmerman from *Ibid.* Reprinted by permission of Unity School of Christianity, Unity Village, Mo.

PHOTOGRAPHERS: Walter Chandoha, *pages 4, 5;* Simon Cherpitel, *pages 48, 49;* Jim Cozad, *pages 52, 53;* Dr. E. R. Degginger, *pages 36, 37;* Joseph Klemovich, *pages 24, 25, 28, 29, 44, 45;* Fred Maroon/Louis Mercier, *pages 60, 61;* David Muench, *pages 8, 9;* H. Armstrong Roberts, *pages 32, 33;* Bob & Ira Spring, *title page.*

Look for the Rainbow

...the night is never

wholly dark,

and no night

is endless....

THE NIGHT IS NOT DARK

They tell of Adam:

How frightened he must have been when, for the first time, he saw the sun disappear, ending the light of day.

It was Adam's first *darkness!*

How could he understand the night, when he had never seen a dawn?

After the splendor of the sun, how astonishingly dark the darkness was; how desperate the long terror of the first fall of night...until Adam learned that *day* would come again: that there is order in the universe.

And then Adam could begin to see how much light *remains* in the sky at night: the stars, and their enduring promise of the sun...

The returning star of day.

Adam learned *the night is never wholly dark, and no night is endless*...even as each of us must learn it in our own times of trouble and of darkness.

The light is never far.

— The Jewish Theological Seminary of America

Mildred Meeker: WINTER HEART

A winter heart is a valiant thing,
Not bound to the summer trill
Of a brook, or a bobolink on the wing,
Or the meadows where daisies spill.

A winter heart can stand the test
When the wind blows wild and high,
And the snows ride down the horizon's crest
From a gray and sunless sky.

For hope beats strong in a winter heart
And nothing can dim its glow,
Though the night be black with winter's art
And the stars refuse to show.

God will grant you a winter heart
To rollick and dream and sing,
If you but have an abiding faith
That winter will turn to spring.

Love

is the creative force

sweeping into

and through

and out of life…

to grow in love

is the only continuity

of which

we can be sure….

William Allen White: MARY IS A NET GAIN

*When columnist William A. White's daughter
Mary died, White wrote a stirring tribute
to her in the Emporia* Gazette.
*He subsequently received thousands of letters
of sympathy. Here is the answer
to one of them:*

My Dear _____

I am not quite sure whether I have acknowl-
edged your kind letter about Mary's death. I have
been slow about it because I have not been up to
letter writing. Not that I have been broken with
grief, but I have not known exactly how to ex-
press my feelings.

Mrs. White and I have none but joyous mem-
ories of Mary. She gave out humor and sunshine
as beaten steel gives out sparks, and all our rec-
ollections of her are merry ones. It is hard to
think of her without smiling, and the very shadow of her face across our hearts brings laughter.
We are not deceiving ourselves about the blow.
It was a terrible stroke and we are infinitely lonely. But we are not shaking the bars of this finite
cage and asking unanswerable questions of fate.
We know that we do not know and that it is all
mysterious. Yet, because our most uncommon

lot of happiness for twenty-seven years has by this cruel circumstance been made the common lot, we are not dubious of God and the decency of man.

Mary is a net gain. To have had her seventeen years, joyous, and rollicking, and wise, and so tremendously human in her weaknesses and in her strength is blessing enough for any parents, and we have no right to ask for more.

I am setting these things down because you were kind enough to write us and because I thought you would like to know how we are going along the hard and lonely trail. Accept our sincere and affectionate gratitude for your kind words. They helped. To know that our friends are with us in spirit is about the only answer to prayer that will be vouchsafed us in this material world. As for the other, we can only hope and trust and be cheerful about it.

Sincerely yours,
William A. White

Christina Rossetti: SONG

When I am dead, my dearest,
   Sing no sad songs for me;
Plant thou no roses at my head,
   Nor shady cypress-tree;
Be the green grass above me
   With showers and dewdrops wet;
And if thou wilt, remember,
   And if thou wilt, forget.

I shall not see the shadows,
   I shall not feel the rain;
I shall not hear the nightingale
   Sing on, as if in pain;
And dreaming through the twilight
   That doth not rise nor set,
Haply I may remember,
   And haply may forget.

William Wordsworth: *from*
INTIMATIONS OF IMMORTALITY

What through the radiance
   which was once so bright
Be now forever taken from my sight,
   Though nothing can bring back the hour
Of splendor in the grass, of glory in the flower;
   We will grieve not, rather find
   Strength in what remains behind;
   In the primal sympathy
   Which having been must ever be;
   In the soothing thoughts that spring
   Out of human suffering;
   In the faith that looks through death,
In years that bring the philosophic mind.

Rose Kennedy:
IT HELPS IF I AM CHEERFUL

*The matriarch of the Kennedy family
is no stranger to grief. She has learned
to accept and suppress her heartaches
for the good of those around her:*

It helps other members of the family if I am cheerful rather than if I were depressed or felt completely beaten. I made up my mind that I wouldn't allow it to conquer me. I think Jackie and Ethel were very wonderful. They have never really distressed us by an undue demonstration of grief or sorrow. They've always maintained poise and equanimity, which makes it easier for everyone.

Teddy's wife, Joan, is so talented in music. She used to play the piano while we sang in the evenings in Hyannis Port. Once, after we had lost Jack, we tried to sing some of the songs that he had liked. One of us got depressed and that was—well, we all collapsed, so we closed the piano quickly and everybody went home. We discontinued our singing after that.

You just keep busy. Some people get bored, and are boring. You keep interested in other people and in different activities....I think to lose a husband when you're young is a very great tragedy — very hard on the girls, on the President's wife and Ethel. It is much more severe and heartbreaking, I think, than for a mother to lose a son. I had a wonderful life with my husband, a very happy and complete life on every level, from every angle.

Martha Smock: NO OTHER WAY

Could we but see the pattern of our days,
We should discern how devious were the ways
By which we came to this, the present time,
This place in life; and we should see the climb
Our soul has made up through the years.
We should forget the hurts, the wanderings, the fears,
The wastelands of our life, and know
That we could come no other way or grow
Into our good without these steps our feet
Found hard to take, our faith found hard to meet.
The road of life winds on, and we like travelers go
From turn to turn until we come to know
The truth that life is endless and that we
Forever are inhabitants of all eternity.

I need but take

    His hand

To see life fair,

to see it

    whole and new,

Touched with

    His matchless glory,

    like a land

Of promise....

Rabbi Hyman Judah Schachtel: FAITH

The solace of faith is not received in an attempt to substitute it for grief, for this cannot be done; the most devout must mourn their dead. Perhaps the greater is one's love for God, the greater is one's love for human beings, and hence the greater is one's grief. The strength that faith gives is, first of all, the strength to mourn; then, the strength to reestablish one's life on a new basis. The comfort that faith brings is through enabling one to accept the real, the here and the now.

Goethe:
from HERMANN AND DOROTHEA

The touching image of death
Presents no horror to the wise
And does not appear as the end
To the devout believer.
The former it forces back into life
And teaches him to act;
The latter is strengthened in the dark hour
By the hope of future salvation;
For both death becomes life.

Henry van Dyke: A NEW STREAM

Poet, essayist and professor Henry van Dyke
penned the following piece
in memory of his deceased son:

Ah, my little Barney, you have gone to follow a new stream,—clear as crystal,—flowing through fields of wonderful flowers that never fade. It is a strange river to Teddy and me; strange and very far away. Some day we shall see it with you; and you will teach us the names of those blossoms that do not wither. But till then, little Barney, the other lad and I will follow the old stream that flows by the woodland fireplace,—your altar.

Rue grows here. Yes, there is plenty of rue. But there is also rosemary, that's for remembrance! And close beside it I see a little heart's ease.

C. S. Lewis: MOURNING

*For those left behind, the period immediately
following the death of a loved one
is the hardest. Author C.S. Lewis writes here
about the time of mourning
that followed the death of his wife:*

Something quite unexpected has happened. It came this morning early. For various reasons, not in themselves at all mysterious, my heart was lighter than it had been for many weeks. For one thing, I suppose I am recovering physically from a good deal of mere exhaustion. And I'd had a very tiring but very healthy twelve hours the day before, and a sounder night's sleep; and after ten days of low-hung grey skies and motionless warm dampness, the sun was shining and there was a light breeze. And suddenly at the very moment when, so far, I mourned H. least, I remembered her best. Indeed it was something (almost) better than memory; an instantaneous, unanswerable impression. To say it was like a meeting would be going too far. Yet there was that in it which tempts one to use those words. It was as if the lifting of the sorrow removed a barrier.

I believe I can make sense out of it. You can't see anything properly while your eyes are blurred with tears. You can't, in most things, get what you want if you want it too desperately: anyway, you can't get the best out of it. 'Now! Let's have a real good talk' reduces everyone to silence, 'I *must* get a good sleep tonight' ushers in hours of wakefulness. Delicious drinks are wasted on a really ravenous thirst. Is it similarly the very intensity of the longing that draws the iron curtain, that makes us feel we are staring into a vacuum when we think about our dead?

And so, perhaps, with God. I have gradually been coming to feel that the door is no longer shut and bolted. Was it my own frantic need that slammed it in my face? The time when there is nothing at all in your soul except a cry for help may be just the time when God can't give it: you are like the drowning man who can't be helped because he clutches and grabs. Perhaps your own reiterated cries deafen you to the voice you hoped to hear....Perhaps your own passion temporarily destroys the capacity.

Then a woman said, Speak to us of Joy and Sorrow.

And he answered:

Your joy is your sorrow unmasked.

And the selfsame well from which your laughter rises was oftentimes filled with your tears.

And how else can it be?

The deeper that sorrow carves into your being, the more joy you can contain.

Is not the cup that holds your wine the very cup that was burned in the potter's oven?

And is not the lute that soothes your spirit the very wood that was hollowed with knives?

When you are joyous, look deep into your heart and you shall find it is only that which has given you sorrow that is giving you joy.

When you are sorrowful, look again in your heart and you shall see that in truth you are weeping for that which has been your delight.

Some of you say, "Joy is greater than sorrow," and others say, "Nay, sorrow is the greater."

But I say unto you, they are inseparable.

Together they come, and when one sits alone with you at your board, remember that the other is asleep upon your bed.

Verily you are suspended like scales between your sorrow and your joy.

Only when you are empty are you at standstill and balanced.

When the treasure-keeper lifts you to weigh his gold and his silver, needs must your joy or your sorrow rise or fall.

Billy Graham: A NEW HORIZON

Death is a departure, not to oblivion but to a new horizon. The Psalmist wrote not of disappearing *into* the "valley of the shadow of death," but of going *through* it. And in his 23rd Psalm, one of the most beautiful passages in all literature, the picture he paints is of a tender shepherd herding his flock through a fearful and unknown place, touching them gently with his rod, as if to say, "Fear no evil, for I am with thee."

"All is of God

that is,

and is to be;

And God is good."

Eleanor Halbrook Zimmerman:
LIFE IS GOOD

Let me not fail to find that life is good.
Though storms may rage around me, and the da
Press close upon the heights whereon I've stood
Let me lift up a song as does the lark
Sure of the warming sunlight when the shower
Is done, and rainbow beauty rims the hill,
For nothing hinders God's almighty power
To summon blessings where and how He will.

From out the stormiest place, the darkest deep,
At His great word a steadfast friend may come,
Or from the loss that once I stayed to weep,
A shining blessing greater than the sum
Of all my woes. I need but take His hand
To see life fair, to see it whole and new,
Touched with His matchless glory, like a land
Of promise such as eager pilgrims view.
I need but trust His love, as all men should,
To know with joy and faith that life is good.

Norman Vincent Peale: INVITATION

One traditional concept that I think we could and should discard is the concept of death as a Grim Reaper, hooded and hostile, stalking mankind with a scythe. It's an ancient tradition, I'll admit; even Shakespeare likens death to a dread sergeant who "is strict in his arrest." But I'm convinced that this is a mistaken notion. The departed person has not been snatched forcibly away, although to the grieving ones left behind it may sometimes seem like that. I prefer to think that he has been given an invitation, and that some deep wisdom in him has decided to accept, that's all.

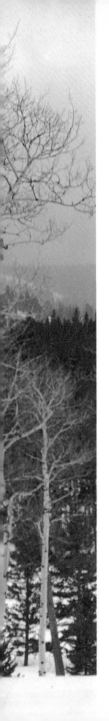

God will grant you

    a winter heart

To rollick

    and dream and sing,

If you but have

    an abiding faith

That winter

    will turn to spring.

Music is a delight because of its rhythm and flow. Yet the moment you arrest the flow and prolong a note or chord beyond its time, the rhythm is destroyed. Because life is likewise a flowing process, change and death are its necessary parts. To work for their exclusion is to work against life.

— Alan W. Watts

Have courage for the great sorrows of life and patience for the small ones. And when you have finished your daily task, go to sleep in peace. God is awake.

—Victor Hugo

Only one principle will give you courage; that is the principle that no evil lasts forever nor indeed for very long.

—Epicurus

Sometimes I go about pitying myself, and all the time I am being carried on great winds across the sky.

—American Indian Saying

Where true serenity and boundless trust in God's goodness prevail, man will not, in spite of cares, give himself over to excessive pain. For we are certain that God is always a wise and good father even when He sends trials and tribulations.

—Nicodemus

Look forward without fear to that appointed hour,— the last hour of the body, but not of the soul....That day, which you fear as being the end of all things, is the birthday of your eternity.

—Seneca

We will

  grieve not,

rather find strength

in what remains

  behind….

From the Taoist Scriptures:
THE DEATH OF CHUANG TZE'S WIFE

When Chuang Tze's wife died, Hui Tze went to offer his sympathy. He found the widower sitting on the ground, singing, with his legs spread out at a right angle, and beating time on a bowl.

"To live with your wife," exclaimed Hui Tze, "and see your eldest son grow up to be a man, and then not to shed a tear over her corpse,— this would be bad enough. But to drum on a bowl and sing; surely this is going too far."

"Not at all," replied Chuang Tze. "When she died, I could not help being affected by her death. Soon, however, I remembered that she had already existed in a previous state before birth, without form, or even substance; that while in that unconditioned condition, substance was added to spirit; that this substance then assumed form; and that the next stage was birth. And now, by virtue of a further change, she is dead, passing from one phase to another like the sequence of spring, summer, autumn, and winter. And while she is thus lying asleep in eternity, for me to go about weeping and wailing would be to proclaim myself ignorant of these natural laws. Therefore I refrain."

William Penn: CROSSING THE WORLD

They that love beyond the world,
cannot be separated by it.

Death cannot kill what never dies.

Nor can spirits ever be divided that
love and live in the same divine principle;
the root and record of their friendship.

If absence be not death, neither is theirs.

Death is but crossing the world, as friends
do the seas; they live in one another still.

For they must needs be present, that
love and live in that which is omnipresent.

In this divine glass they see face to face;
and their converse is free as well
as pure.

This is the comfort of friends, that
though they may be said to die, yet their
friendship and society are in the best
sense ever present, because immortal.

Have courage

for the

great sorrows of life

and patience

for the small ones....

Helen Hayes:
THE LARGER TRUTH

*Actress Helen Hayes lost her daughter Mary
and her husband, Charles MacArthur, only
a few months apart. She recounts that trying
time in her autobiography* On Reflection:

Mary and I were appearing together in *Good
Housekeeping* up at Westport, Connecticut,
when she caught the cold that turned out to be
polio. Her fatigue seemed excessive and I sent
her home to Nyack against her will.

Charlie was at the Lenox Hill Hospital being
treated for his ulcers, and a few days after her
return she joined him across the hall—still in-
sisting that I stay with the play and open in
Bucks County, where she would then rejoin me.

Charlie, at first agreeing with her, now called
me when the doctor became suspicious. I
closed the play and rushed to New York, where
I found Mary in an iron lung.

It isn't reasonable to outlive one's child. It is
against everything natural, but it happens. It
happened to us. Our Mary lost her battle a few
days later. She was 19....Charlie became stronger
than he had ever been when he saw me sway.

He became my bastion until I regained my balance. When I did, he stumbled—never to right himself again. He had rallied for me and this last, great burst of energy was too much for his sick body and tired soul.

He now started his tragic pursuit of the blithe spirit who was our daughter. His decline was slow, but steady—his holidays from reality more extended, his periods of productivity dwindling simply to talk. His powers were ebbing and I watched my husband grow old before my eyes: not imperceptibly, so that one day you say of some unchanging friend, in a moment of illumination, "Heavens, when did he become old?"; but, rather, overnight—in a shocking dissolve.

We never seemed to be strong together—at the same time—except when we were fresh in love and fighting the forces that would have kept us apart. For that, I will always be grateful. How terrible it would have been to have missed my life with him.

As battles are lost and wars still won, there were admittedly regrettable moments in my marriage, but they do not alter the larger truth. Charlie MacArthur and I had found each other in the crowd—he never stopped calling me his bride. That miracle remains.

And now Charlie started dying, when he was certain that I would survive.

I visited Mary's grave one winter's day recently, with a birthday bouquet of her favorite flowers. They had been her first present from a gentleman, that bouquet she'd received the first day of her life from her father.

When I arrived at the cemetery, I found that a recent snow had left such drifts that the path to Mary was impassable. After circling the area and testing the crustiness of the snow's surface, I could only give up after landing knee-deep in one of the shallower approaches.

Terribly disappointed, I looked at the bunch of violets that circled the one red rose and refused to be daunted. They were for Mary and, by gum, Mary was going to have them. Taking careful aim, I pitched the flowers across the great drift and they landed—a brilliant explosion of color—on the frozen grave. *Daddy would have been proud of me,* I thought. It was a pitch worthy of Walter Johnson.

The absurdity of the moment would have delighted Mary. I knew that. It suddenly struck me funny as well. It was the first laugh my daughter and I shared in many years, and I was refreshed by it.

Rowena Cheney: WINGS

Silent wings above my head—
    A shadow on the earth below;
I had not known the bird was there
    But for that motion on the snow.

Sometimes a shadow on life's path
    May bid us pause to look above
And find, outspread against the sky,
    The quiet, sheltering wings of love.

Helen Papashvily: A NEW PERSPECTIVE

*Writing about her immigrant husband's
experiences as a boy, author Helen Papashvily
touches upon a truth of life
that too few people ever understand:*

When George was a little boy in the Caucasus he was taken once to visit a revered old man who lived all alone, high on a mountaintop.

It was customary for each child in the district to give the hermit a gift and receive in return a special proverb or word of advice that he might use as a talisman thereafter through his future life.

The old man had a stern face and a long white beard. He beckoned the boy to come closer. George was frightened but he went. The old man waved the grown people away and then...asked the little boy at his side what he wanted to do and where he wanted to go when he was grown. He told him tales of his own life and his travels over the earth.

After a little while he said, "Now to give you your proverb. I want it to be something that will be of use to you when you are young and when you are old—something to help when you feel sad or tired or discouraged—something to remember when you doubt and fear."

George waited.

The old man bent down and whispered in his ear, "This minute, too, is part of eternity."

George didn't understand it (perhaps he wasn't meant to) until he grew up. For like many simple truths it needs thought and re-flection and experience to make it clear.

But once comprehended it affords a whole new perspective of life with vistas as wide as space and as long as time. The simplest act acquires dignity and import; the most fleeting moment, meaning. Birth and death, instead of being two irreconcilable parts, form a harmoni-ous whole.

As the clouds of despair

begin to disperse,

you realize

that there is hope,

and life, and light,

and truth.

There is goodness

in the universe....

John Greenleaf Whittier:
ALL IS OF GOD THAT IS

The same old baffling questions! O my friend,
I cannot answer them. In vain I send
My soul into the dark, where never burn
The lamps of science, nor the natural light
Of Reason's sun and stars! I cannot learn
Their great and solemn meanings, nor discern
The awful secrets of the eyes which turn
Evermore on us through the day and night
With silent challenge and a dumb demand,
Proffering the riddles of the dread unknown,
Like the calm Sphinxes, with their eyes of stone
Questioning the centuries from their veils of san
I have no answer for myself or thee,
Save that I learned beside my mother's knee;
"All is of God that is, and is to be;
And God is good." Let this suffice us still.
Resting in childlike trust upon His will
Who moves to His great ends unthwarted
                                        by the ill.

Coretta Scott King:
THE GOOD FRIDAYS OF LIFE

Dr. Martin Luther King, Jr., was assassinated
in Memphis in April of 1968. Yet his wife
did not consider his death a total tragedy:

Martin had often talked of the meaning of Easter in human life. He would say that the moments of despair and doubt were the Good Fridays of life. But, Martin always added, even in the darkest moments, something happens, and you hear the drums of Easter. As the clouds of despair begin to disperse, you realize that there is hope, and life, and light, and truth. There is goodness in the universe. That is what Martin saw as the meaning of Easter.

The road of life

    winds on, and we

        like travelers go

From turn to turn

until we come to know

The truth

    that life is endless....

Elizabeth Yates: AN OPEN LETTER

When writer Elizabeth Yates' husband died,
instead of allowing her grief to ruin
her life, she set down her innermost thoughts
in this open letter to anyone who had shared
her heartache. Her words of encouragement
have helped thousands of people to overcome
their sorrow and accept the will of God:

My Dear:

This may be quite a long letter, for there is so much that I want to share with you.... Miles apart as we are, our thoughts will be meeting, and it will almost be as if we were clasping hands.

My heart has ached for you in the loss that has come in your life, and my affection has reached out to embrace you in the bright busy hours of the day and even more in the still, lonely hours of the night. This sorrow that has brought us close together makes us one with every person who has ever known sorrow. This can be a kind of special blessing to us all, right now....

No matter how brave we think we are, or think we can be, we must call sorrow by its right name and see it for what it is. Only then can we avail ourselves of the treasure that is hidden in the folds of its dark cloak. I think that we should not, by any twist of the words we use, minimize what we are going through, what anyone goes through, when death enters upon life and removes a member of our circle, family-close or friendship-wide....A light has gone out; wherever it may be shining, it is here no longer.

Face the dark night then, as a night, but with the knowledge that there is no night so long that dawn does not sometimes end it. When the day comes we shall face it, too, stronger and wiser and, if our prayers have had any breadth to them, far more compassionate. Only those who have gone through a comparable experience know what struggling, what searching, what grasping goes on in the dark.

With growing things, day and night, light and dark all serve nature's purpose, as does the cold of winter, the warmth of summer, sun and rain and wind. So much of the work essential to growing is done in the dark, unseen, unnoticed, until the visible evidence of shoot or stalk or sprout appears to break through the crust of earth. Then, with roots established and capable of continuing their holding and their reaching, the top begins to reach in a different way....

Think with me for a moment: no matter how

"This minute, too,

is part

of eternity."

we enjoy the company of a friend, how we delight in the warmth of good comradeship, there are significant parts of every day that are spent alone. Inner growing and aspiring, even a certain amount of daily doing and planning, are all prompted by or become the result of those times of aloneness. In the quiet times deliberately sought, or in those enforced upon us, we discover ideas that can be put to use when we return again to the busy world of people. If the loneliness is deeper now, it may be that more may be found within it.

Barrie gave brave words to Peter Pan when, alone on the rock as the rising waters were coming nearer, the boy who never wanted to grow up flung back his head and cried, "To die must be an awfully big adventure." And of that we have no slightest doubt; yet, for the one who is left to live on in life, it is an equally big adventure.

But—

Can we ever tell, as we stand at the threshold of a new day, just what the day will bring? No matter how carefully planned the hours may be, or how wisely plotted the duties, there are always openings, and through them may come a promise of friendship, a glimpse of beauty, a coin of wisdom's minting, a high clear call of glory. In bed at night, before falling asleep, to go back over the day and weigh the unexpected against the prepared is to realize that there has been more of the former than the latter. There may be a condition here: the courageous spirit and the questing mind are always having adventures. To be ready for the unexpected is to find it waiting—in people, in places, in daily events: and...to use and profit by what is encountered.

This I know: my dear one has gone closer to God. This, too, I know: that as I live close to God I shall be near him. Death has made me only more sure of my connectedness. It is in God we live and in God we meet at last. To indulge personal sorrow or the sense of loneliness will not help toward this meeting, but serenity will, and discipline, and inner gladness, and the willingness to yield to the new demands. I have learned that when I keep my life right—and by that I mean responsive, gay, creative, giving—I am most near to my dear one because I am most near to God. If I allow myself to become heavyhearted I find that I am a long way from him, and it is a weary while to get myself back.

Often in my reading, I find that what I am trying to say to you has been said so much better by someone else, and so I give you Amiel's words—

The eternal life is not the future life; it is life in harmony with the true order of things—life in God. We must learn to look upon time as a movement of eternity, as an undulation in the ocean of being. To live, so as to keep this consciousness of ours in perpetual relation with the eternal, is to be wise; to live, so as to personify and embody the eternal, is to be religious.

Sometime or another each one of us will face aloneness. It was only when I did that I began to learn the real meaning of the word that I had read, heard, used for years as part of the English language. It does not matter how rich and rare and satisfying the relationships we have known have been—in families, in friendship, in work, in marriage—there comes a time when each one must see himself as an integer in the Universe: not dependent on or conjoined with anyone else, not needed by or needing anyone else. Something begins to happen then. The only way I know how to say it is that we become aware as never before of our relationship with God, and the actual definition of the word alone— *All plus one*— has a personal meaning.

When this began to work itself through to me, I was acutely conscious of the one; only gradually could I accept the All. But, in time, it became like a great protective mountain rising behind me.

One day, when I was about ten years old and walking home from school, I stopped to read some words on the notice board outside a church. The capsule sermons lettered there week after week always drew my attention and gave me much to ponder. But these words puzzled me. It was hard to make any sense out of them—

And we are put on earth a little space,

That we may learn to bear the beams of love.

How could something like love that was warm and comforting, as I had always known it to be, be heavy like a piece of wood?

The words lodged in my mind.... They have been speaking to me ever since, but never more clearly than this past year and on one particular occasion when they helped me to grasp a point being made by an astronomer in the course of a lecture.... In the midst of all the weighty presentation, the astronomer used the phrase "communication on a beam of light." Suddenly, I knew exactly what he was talking about, but I'm sure that I would not have known had it not been for the discovery that I have made this past year: that love is the link, invisible as the light and strong as the beam; that love is the creative force sweeping into and through and out of life; and that to grow in love is the only continuity of which we can be sure.

Love is the adventure, as it is the challenge and the test. There is nothing new about this. Others have said it; others will say it again. But each one of us has to make the discovery and say it in our own way that it may become valid in our lives.

This has been a long letter. I think it is time now for me to close and say,

God's blessing on you.

Alfred, Lord Tennyson: PERFECT LOVE

Ye be comforted;
For if this earth be ruled by Perfect Love,
Then, after his brief range of blameless days
The toll of funeral in an Angel ear
Sounds happier than the merriest marriage bell.

The face of Death is toward the Sun of Life,
His shadow darkens earth; his truer name
Is "Onward," no discordance in the roll
And march of that Eternal Harmony
Whereto the worlds beat time, tho' faintly heard
Until the great Hereafter. Mourn in hope.

God of our fathers
and our God,
give us the faith
to believe
in the ultimate triumph
of righteousness....
We pray
for the bifocals of faith
that see the despair
and the need of the hour
but also see,
further on,
the patience of our God
working out His plan
in the world
He has made....
Through Jesus our Lord.
AMEN.   PETER MARSHALL

Set in Crown, designed exclusively
for Hallmark Editions by Hermann Zapf.
Typography by Hallmark Photo Composition.
Printed on Hallmark Crown Royale paper.